PUPIL WORKBOOK

YEAR 1

Contents

Properties and uses of materials

Animals (vertebrates)

Identifying plants and their parts

Module 1

Seasonal changes

Date: ____________________

The lessons in this module take place at different points of the year.

Talk about the answers to these questions with a partner.

Where you live, do these things change throughout the year? Tick (✓) Yes or No.

The weather and temperature: Yes ☐ No ☐

The plants and flowers you see: Yes ☐ No ☐

The birds you see: Yes ☐ No ☐

The animals you see: Yes ☐ No ☐

Lesson 1 Are all leaves the same?

Key vocabulary

leaf/leaves plant season

Date: ____________________

Activity 1: Today's weather and length of day

Tick (✓) to show what the weather is like today.

Circle the correct word. Yesterday, it was light / dark when I went to bed.

Today, it was light / dark when I got up.

Activity 2: My leaf

You will need

- a leaf
- white paper
- a crayon
- scissors
- glue

- Look closely at your leaf and feel different parts of it with your fingers.
- Circle the words in the box that describe your leaf.
- Cover your leaf with the paper. Gently rub with the crayon.
- Cut out your leaf rubbing and stick it here.

rough	smooth
shiny	dull
furry	spiky
jagged	frilly
bumpy	wrinkly

Look at your partner's leaf. How is it the same as your leaf? How is it different?

Activity 3: Which plant did my leaf come from?

- Find the plant your leaf comes from.
- Look in books or look where you found your leaf. Ask an adult to help.
- Draw the plant here and write its name. ____________________

Are all the leaves on the plant the same? Tick (✓) one. Yes ☐ No ☐

Activity 4: Seasonal tree

Write the name of the **season** it is today.

____

Circle words in the box to describe the weather today.

hot	wet	very hot	sunny
rainy	cloudy	windy	cold

Find a tree near your home or school or use the one in the picture here.

A horse chestnut tree

Are the leaves on the tree the same or different to the leaf you looked at in Activity 1?

Tick (✓) one. Same ☐ Different ☐

How are the leaves different to your leaf from Activity 1? Tell your partner.

Are all leaves the same?

Tick (✓) one. Yes ☐ No ☐

Key learning

In this lesson I have learnt that: Different **plants** have different **leaves**. Leaves can be different colours, shapes, sizes and textures. In some countries, leaves can look different at different times of year.

Homework

Collect leaves with different colours and shapes. Use them to make a picture.

Lesson 2 Which animals share our space?

Key vocabulary

animal autumn bird season

Date: ________________

Activity 1: Today's weather and length of day

Tick (✓) to show what the weather is like today.

Circle the correct word.

Yesterday, it was light / dark when I went to bed.

Today, it was light / dark when I got up.

Activity 2: Signs of autumn

Are these autumn pictures different to where you live? How is it different?

The **autumn** season is different in different places in the world. In some places, the weather gets colder and leaves fall from the trees.

Look at the photographs and talk to a partner. What can you see that are signs of autumn?

Activity 3: Which animals live near me?

Go on a nature walk. Afterwards, tick (✓) the things that you saw.

Animal	Animal clues
☐ spider	☐ web
☐ worm	☐ worm cast
☐ butterfly	☐ insect egg
☐ bird	☐ bird's egg
☐ snail	☐ shell
☐ bee	☐ caterpillar

Draw or write the names of other things you saw.

Activity 4: What did you find on your walk?

What did you find on your walk?

Complete these sentences.

I saw lots of ______________________________

I did not see many ______________________________

I did not see any ______________________________

I found a ______________ by the ______________________

I found a ______________ under the ______________________

Key learning

In this lesson I have learnt that: In some countries, the seasons change. When the **seasons** change, the weather can change. Days get longer or shorter and trees can look different. You might see different **birds** and other **animals** in different seasons.

Homework

Look for animal clues. For example, a footprint, an egg, a shell. Make a note of what you find and which animal you think left the clue. You could take a photograph to show to the class.

Do all trees shed their leaves?

Key vocabulary

deciduous	leaf/leaves	season
evergreen	tree	winter

Date: ________________

Activity 1: Today's weather and length of day

Tick (✓) to show what the weather is like today.

FOG

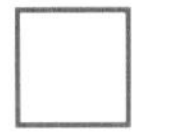

Circle the correct word.

Yesterday, it was light / dark when I went to bed.

Today, it was light / dark when I got up.

Activity 2: Signs of winter

Are these winter pictures different to where you live? How is it different?

The winter season is different in different places in the world. This picture shows a winter scene.

Look at the photographs and talk to a partner. What can you see that are signs of winter?

Activity 3: Evergreen or deciduous?

Some trees have leaves in the summer but not in the winter. These trees are called deciduous trees.

Some trees have green leaves all year. These trees are called evergreen trees.

Use the pictures on page 9 to write the names of the trees in the boxes below.

Can you find out about another evergreen and deciduous tree?

Evergreen	Deciduous

I can tell if a tree is evergreen or deciduous by ______________________________

____

____

Key learning

In this lesson I have learnt that: In some countries, the **season** changes to **winter**. The weather gets colder and days get shorter. Some **trees** lose their **leaves**. We call these trees **deciduous**. Some trees have leaves all year. We call these trees **evergreen**.

Homework

Find a deciduous tree and an evergreen tree (in a book or near your house). Compare them. Write about what is the same and what is different.

Lesson 4 Are all flowers the same?

Key vocabulary

flower petal spring

Date: ______________

Activity 1: Today's weather and length of day

Tick (✓) to show what the weather is like today.

☐ ☐ ☐ ☐ ☐ ☐

Circle the correct word.

Yesterday, it was light / dark when I went to bed.

Today, it was light / dark when I got up.

Activity 2: Signs of spring

Are these spring pictures different to where you live? How is it different?

In some countries, the season changes to spring. In spring, the weather gets warmer and the days get longer. Lots of plants change in spring.

Look at the photographs and talk to a partner. What happens to plants in spring?

Activity 3: Comparing flowers

- Look at your flower.
- Draw one of the petals.
- Write a sentence to describe the colour and shape of the petal.

You will need

- a flower

____

____

____

Draw the whole flower.

petunia

Compare the photo of the petunia flower to your flower. Complete the sentences below.

The flowers are the same because they both ______________________________

____

The flowers are different because my flower ______________________________ but

the petunia flower ______________________________

Activity 4: Flower colours in spring

Go on a flower hunt near your home or school.

For each flower you see, tick (✓) the matching colour.

white		yellow	
orange		red	
pink		purple	
blue		green	

Complete this sentence:

The most common colour of flower was ______________________

Circle the correct answer to complete the sentence.

All flowers are the same / different.

Key learning

In this lesson I have learnt that: In some countries, the season changes to **spring**. In spring, the weather gets warmer and the days get longer. Lots of **flowers** bloom in spring. Their **petals** can be different colours and shapes.

Homework

Make a flower using materials you find outside.

Lesson 5 Which birds can we spot?

Key vocabulary

bird nest spring

Date: ____________

Activity 1: Today's weather and length of day

Tick (✓) to show what the weather is like today.

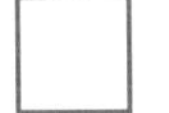

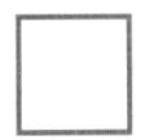

Circle the correct word.

Yesterday, it was light / dark when I went to bed.

Today, it was light / dark when I got up.

Activity 2: Signs of spring

Are these spring pictures different to where you live? How is it different?

In some countries, the season changes to spring. In spring, the weather gets warmer and the days get longer. Lots of animals are born in spring.

Look at the photographs and talk to a partner. What can you see that tells you it is spring?

Activity 3: Bird spotting

- Look for birds near your home or school. You must be very quiet and still!
- Fill in the information below for a bird you saw, or for one of the birds in the pictures.

magpie

wood pigeon

robin

starling

house sparrow

Colour of feathers ______________________________

Colour of beak ______________________________

Shape of beak ______________________________

Colour of legs ______________________________

The bird lives ______________________________

Circle the feet that are the best match to the feet of the bird you have chosen.

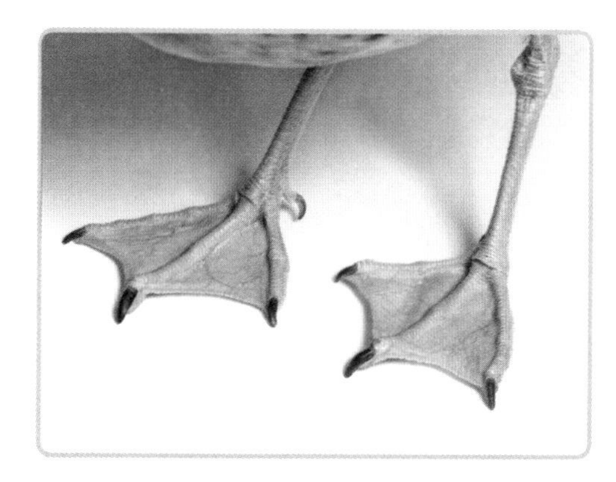

Activity 4: Comparing birds

Choose another bird that you saw, or another bird from the last activity.

Write the name of a bird that you saw ______________________________

What colour was it? ______________________________

What was its beak like? ______________________________

What else did you notice? ______________________________

Draw a picture of your bird and add labels.

Find someone who drew a different bird than you. Discuss the questions.

How is your bird the same as your partner's bird?

How is your bird different to your partner's bird?

Our birds are similar because ...

Our birds are different because ...

Activity 5: Counting birds

- Look for more birds near your school or house.
- For each bird you see, tick (✓) to show where you saw it.

On a plant	On the ground	In the air	In water	Somewhere else

I saw most of the birds ___________________________

Key learning

In this lesson I have learnt that: Different **birds** have different coloured feathers, feet and beaks. We see different types of bird at different times of the year. Some birds build **nests** in **spring**.

Homework

Build a bird's nest using found materials. For example, dried grasses, twigs and fallen leaves. Where would you put the nest to keep the eggs safe?

Lesson 6 How has our space changed over the year?

Key vocabulary

flower summer weather

Date: ______________

Activity 1: Today's weather and length of day

Tick (✓) to show what the weather is like today.

Circle the correct word.

Yesterday, it was light / dark when I went to bed.

Today, it was light / dark when I got up.

Activity 2: Signs of summer

Are these summer pictures different to where you live? How is it different?

In many countries, summer is the hottest time of the year.

Look at the photographs and talk to a partner. How do you know that it is summer?

Activity 3: Flower colours in summer

Go on a **flower** hunt. Look in the area around you, or look in the pictures below.

For each flower you see, tick (✓) the matching colour.

white		yellow		orange	
red		pink		purple	
blue		green			

Complete this sentence:

The most common colour of flower was ______________________________

This is different / the same as the flowers in the spring.

Activity 4: Changes in the year

Think about how the area you live in has changed throughout the year. Or use the pictures of seasons in this book and write about them instead. Write or draw your ideas below.

In the autumn I saw ...	**In the winter I saw ...**
In the spring I saw ...	**In the summer I saw ...**

Complete the sentence. My favourite season is ______________________________

because ____

____

Activity 5: Weather and length of day

Look back at the first page of each lesson.

Did the weather change over the year? Tick (✓) one. Yes ☐ No ☐

Did the length of the day change over the year? Tick (✓) one. Yes ☐ No ☐

Activity 6: Season match

Draw or write something that makes you think of each season.

autumn	**winter**
spring	**summer**

Key learning

In this lesson I have learnt that: In countries where there are seasons, the **weather** in **summer** is usually hot and sunny. It is when the days are longest.

Homework

Make a simple butterfly feeder. Place small pieces of over-ripe fruit on a small dish. Put it outside. Draw a picture of any butterflies or other insects that visit.

Module 2

Human body and senses

Lesson 1 Is everyone's body the same?

Key vocabulary

arm	hand	neck	sight
brain	head	sense	torso
foot	leg		

Activity 1: Labelling body parts

- Draw a line to match each word to the body part.
- Add two more labels for neck and leg.

head

torso

arm

hand

foot

Activity 2: The sense of sight

Add the labels to the picture.

eye	nose	mouth	ear

____

____

____

____

How do you see? Talk to a partner.

Fill in the gaps in the sentence. Use the words in the box.

brain	sight	see	eyes

Humans have five senses: ____________, touch, hearing, smell and taste. We use our ____________ to see. Our eyes send messages to our ____________. Our brain helps us to understand what we ____________.

Activity 3: Are all bodies the same?

Are all bodies the same?
Talk to a partner.

Tick (✓) to show whether these parts of the body are usually the same for most people, or often different.

	Usually the same	Often different
Number of legs	☐	☐
Hair colour	☐	☐
Number of toes	☐	☐
Height	☐	☐
Skin colour	☐	☐
Foot size	☐	☐
Number of hands	☐	☐
Eye colour	☐	☐

Key learning

In this lesson I have learnt that: The main parts of our bodies are: **head**, **torso**, **arms** and **hands**, and **legs** and **feet**. We have five **senses**. One of these is **sight**. We use our eyes to see. Our eyes send messages to our **brain** to help us understand what we are seeing. Bodies are not all the same, even though some parts of the body are usually the same.

Homework

Some people cannot see very well. Find out about some things that can help them, such as guide dogs.

Lesson 2 How can we explore the world using our sense of touch?

Key vocabulary

brain sense touch

Activity 1: Exploring the world

How do babies find out about the world around them? Talk to a partner.

What parts of the body do you use to find out about the world around you?

____

Activity 2: Feely feet

You will need

- a blindfold
- a tray containing different objects

- Put on a blindfold (or close your eyes).
- Use your bare feet to feel the objects in the tray.
- Tell a partner how each object feels.
- Tick (✓) the words that you used.

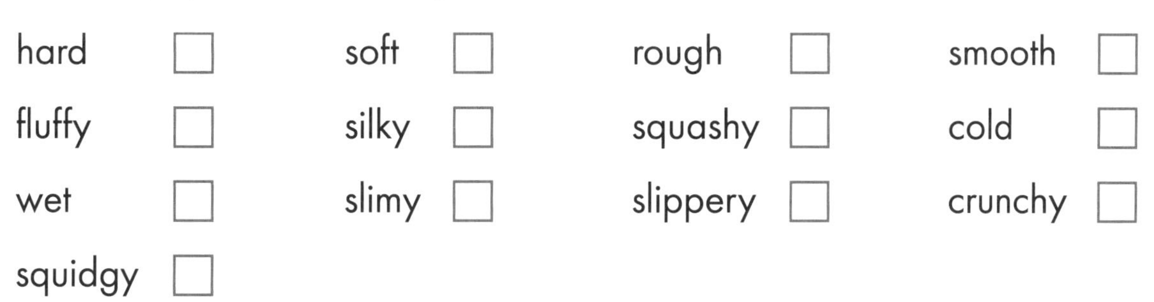

hard	☐	soft	☐	rough	☐	smooth	☐
fluffy	☐	silky	☐	squashy	☐	cold	☐
wet	☐	slimy	☐	slippery	☐	crunchy	☐
squidgy	☐						

Write any other words that you used to describe how the materials felt. ______________

____

Activity 3: Feely bags

You will need

- six numbered 'feely bags' (drawstring bags that you cannot see through)
- a different object hidden inside each bag

- Feel the object inside each bag. Don't look!
- Fill in the table. Use the words in the box to help.

Bag	What does the object feel like?	What do you think it is?
1		
2		
3		
4		
5		
6		

hard	soft	rough
smooth	bumpy	wrinkled
grooved	sticky	crunchy
slippery	spiky	

Activity 4: Warm and cold

- Use parts of your body to feel each object.
- Draw or write the name of the object.
- Use the scale to show how cold or warm it felt using each body part.

You will need

- three different objects, including one warm and one cold

		COLD ⟷ WARM
OBJECT 1	fingertips	
	back of wrist	
	cheek	
	forehead	
OBJECT 2	fingertips	
	back of wrist	
	cheek	
	forehead	
OBJECT 3	fingertips	
	back of wrist	
	cheek	
	forehead	

Complete the sentences. My ______________________________ was / were best at feeling hot and cold.

My ______________________________ was worst at feeling hot and cold.

Key learning

In this lesson I have learnt that: **Touch** is one of our five **senses**. We can feel things with any part of our skin. Our skin sends messages to our **brain** to help us understand what we are feeling.

Homework

Show an adult how objects can feel different using different body parts.

Lesson 3 What can we hear?

Key vocabulary

brain hearing sense

Activity 1: Everyday sounds

Complete the sentences.

We have explored two senses so far. These are ____________ and ____________ .

Now we will explore another sense called hearing.

I use my ____________ to hear.

Look at these pictures. Imagine the sound for each picture.

1 truck

3 bird

2 wind

4 thunder

Answer the questions below. Write the numbers or copy the words.

Which of the sounds have you heard before? ____________

Which of the sounds is loudest? ____________

Which of the sounds is quietest? ____________

Activity 2: Sound walk

- Go on a sound walk around school.
- Write or draw the objects that made the sounds you hear.

Complete the sentences.

The loudest sound was ______________________________

____

The quietest sound was ______________________________

____

There were lots of different sounds in ______________________________

____

There were only a few sounds in ______________________________

____

Key learning

In this lesson I have learnt that: **Hearing** is one of our five **senses**. We use our ears to hear sounds. Our ears send messages to our **brain** to help us understand what we are hearing.

Homework

How many different sounds can you hear on your way home tonight? What sounds do you hear on the way to school tomorrow morning? Are any of these sounds the same?

Lesson 4 What smells do we like and dislike?

Key vocabulary

brain nose sense smell

Activity 1: What body parts do you know now?

Add labels for other body parts you know. Use the words to help you.

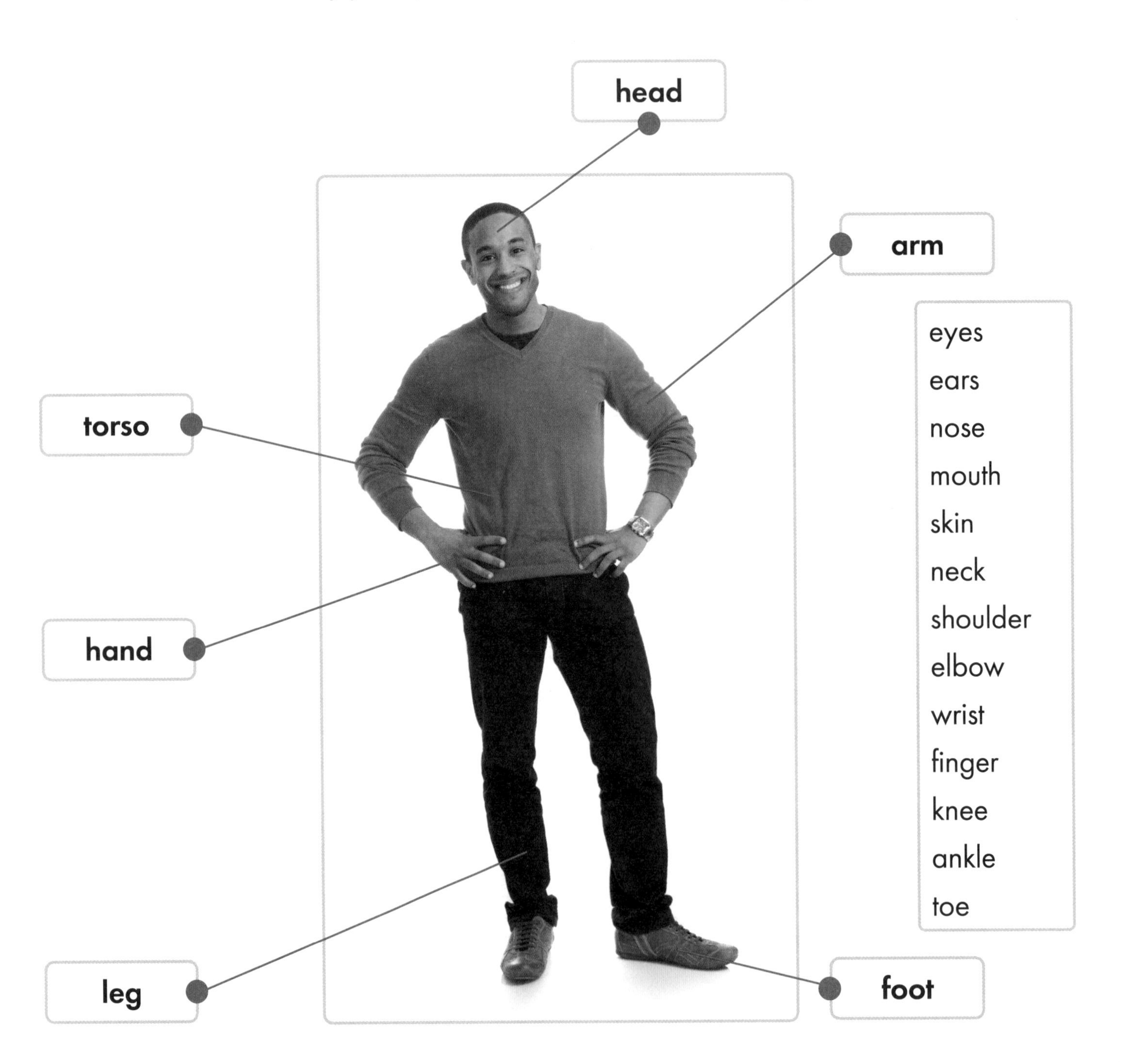

Activity 2: Which smells do we like and dislike?

- Work in a group of four.
- Write your names in the table.
- Smell each pot.
- Record who likes and dislikes each smell.
- Draw ☺ or ☹.

You will need

- four numbered 'smelly pots' (pots each containing a different strong-smelling item)

	Name:	**Name:**	**Name:**	**Name:**
Pot 1				
Pot 2				
Pot 3				
Pot 4				

After you have finished the test, find out what is in each pot. Write it on the chart.

Complete the sentences.

Most people in my group like ______________________________

Fewest people in my group like ______________________________

Most people in my class like ______________________________

Fewest people in my class like ______________________________

The part of my body I use to smell is my ______________________________

Key learning

In this lesson I have learnt that: **Smell** is one of our five **senses**. We use our **nose** to smell. Our nose sends messages to our **brain** to help us understand what we are smelling.

Homework

Find different smells at home. Finds smells you like and smells you don't like.

Lesson 5 What differences can our tongues taste?

Key vocabulary

brain	sense	smell	tongue
hearing	sight	taste	touch

Activity 1: How do we sense things?

Match the senses with the body parts.

sight	ears	+	brain
hearing	nose	+	brain
touch	eyes	+	brain
smell	tongue	+	brain
taste	skin	+	brain

Activity 2: Taste testing

You will need
- lemon juice
- sugar
- a spoon
- small samples of other sweet and sour foods

- Taste drops of lemon juice.
- Taste grains of sugar.
- Next, taste some different types of sweet or sour food.
- In the table, draw or write what you are testing.
- Record how sour or sweet it tastes.

What are you testing?	How sour or sweet is it?	
	Sour like a lemon?	Sweet like sugar?

Key learning

In this lesson I have learnt that: The five human **senses** are **sight**, **touch**, **hearing**, **smell** and **taste**. We use our **tongue** to taste. Our tongue sends messages to our **brain** to help us understand what we are tasting.

Homework

Make a note of a food you eat at home that tastes sweet, and a food that tastes sour.

Module 3

Naming and describing materials

Lesson 1 What material is this? Part 1

Key vocabulary

manufactured materials natural properties

Activity 1: Wood, metal or plastic?

- Find objects made from wood, metal and plastic. Sort them into groups. Talk about them to a partner.
- Write the material: metal, wood or plastic.

____

____

____

How are the metal objects different from the wooden ones? Use your senses to help.

____

____

____

How are the plastic objects different from the metal and wooden ones? Use your senses to help.

Write the name of two more objects made from each material.

Wood: _______________ _______________

Metal: _______________ _______________

Plastic: _______________ _______________

Activity 2: Comparing objects

The words to describe a material are its properties.

hard	soft	stiff	bendy
smooth	rough	light	heavy

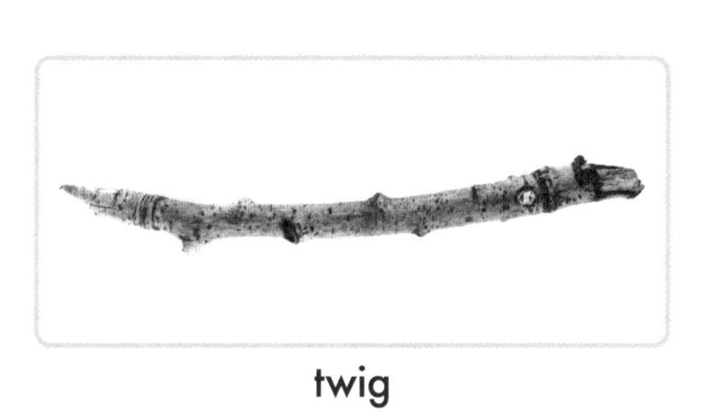

twig

table

Use the words to finish the sentences.

The twig and the table are similar because they are both ______________________

____

The twig and the table are different because the twig is ______________ but the table is ______________________

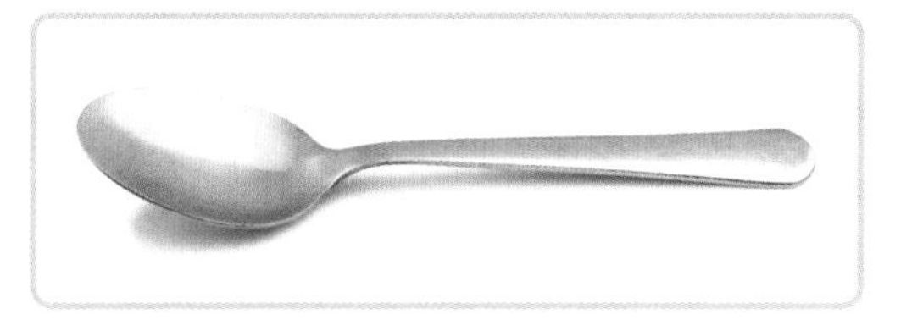

metal spoon

plastic spoon

Use the words to finish the sentences.

The spoons are similar because they are both ______________________

____

The spoons are different because the metal spoon is ______________ but the plastic spoon is ______________________

Activity 3: Natural or manufactured?

Draw lines to show whether each material is natural or manufactured.

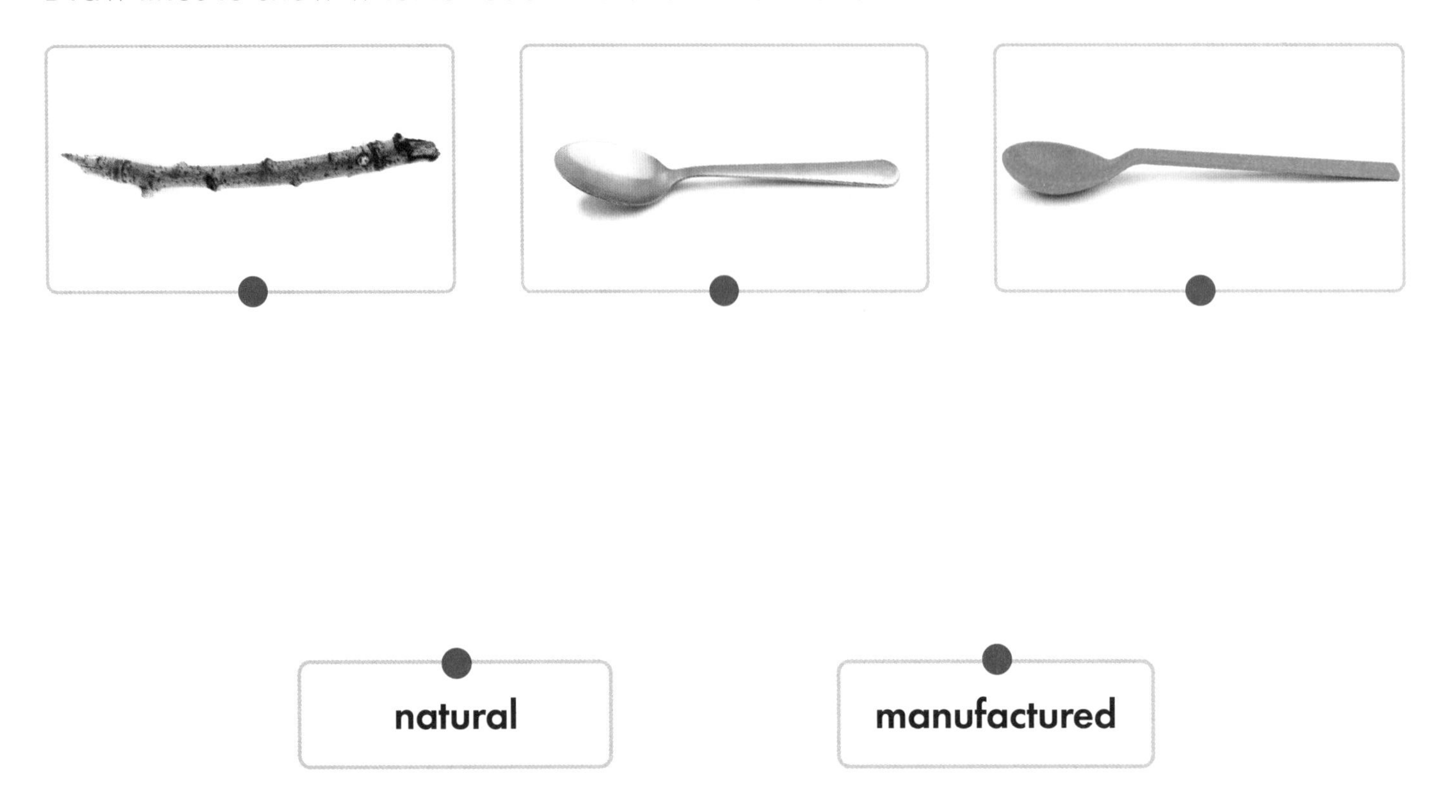

Key learning

In this lesson I have learnt that: Everything around us is made of **materials**. Some materials are **natural**. Some are **manufactured**. A manufactured material is a natural material that has been changed into a new material. Different materials have different **properties**.

Homework

Find three objects at home: one made of wood, one made of metal and one made of plastic. Draw or photograph the objects, or bring them into school. Think about their properties and write words to describe them.

Lesson 2 What material is this? Part 2

Key vocabulary

flexible	material	properties	transparent
fragile	natural	recycled	
manufactured	opaque	rigid	

Activity 1: Describing glass, rock, brick and water

You will need

- an object made of glass
- a brick
- rock samples
- water

- Look at each object.
- Write some words to describe each material.
- Use the words in the box to help you.

glass

____

____

rock

____

____

brick

____

____

water

____

____

hard
soft
shiny
dull
smooth
rough
wet
dry
opaque
transparent
heavy
light
rigid
flexible
strong
fragile

Activity 2: Rock and brick

Use a magnifier to look closely at the brick and rock samples.

Draw what you can see through the magnifier.

How does the magnifier help you to observe the rocks?

You will need

- a brick
- two rock samples
- a magnifier

brick	rock 1	rock 2

Activity 3: Glass, water, rock or brick?

Write the name of the material: glass, water, rock or brick.

__________ __________ __________ __________

__________ __________ __________ __________

Write the name of two more objects made from each material.

glass: __________ __________

water: __________ __________

rock: __________ __________

brick: __________ __________

Activity 4: What material is this?

Write the material: wood, plastic, metal, glass, water, rock or brick.

What should you do with materials that cannot be used more than once?

- Circle the materials that can be used more than once.
- Tick (✓) the materials that cannot be used more than once.

Key learning

In this lesson I have learnt that: Rock and water are **natural materials**. Brick and glass are **manufactured**. Different materials have different **properties**. For example, water and glass are **transparent**. Rock and brick are **opaque**. Materials should be used carefully. They can often be reused or **recycled**.

Homework

Look for these materials in your local environment: wood, plastic, glass, metal, water and rock. Take photographs, write a list or draw some examples to share in school.

Lesson 3 Is all paper the same?

Key vocabulary

absorb/absorbent
manufactured
material
natural
property/properties
recycle
reuse

Activity 1: The paper test

You are going to carry out some tests.

You will test five different types of paper, to find out how good they are for:

1. painting a face on
2. writing your name in pencil on
3. writing your name in coloured marker pen on
4. writing your name in wax crayon on
5. soaking up water from a pipette.

Record your results in the table.

You will need

- five different types of paper
- watercolour paint
- a paintbrush
- a pencil
- a coloured marker pen
- a wax crayon
- a pipette
- water

How did you decide which was the best?

How did you decide which was the worst?

For each task, write 'B' for the paper that is best, and 'W' for the paper that is worst.

Type of paper	Task				
	Painting	Writing (pencil)	Writing (marker)	Writing (crayon)	Mopping up water

Activity 2: What did you find out?

Complete each sentence.

The paper that was best for painting was ____________________

It was best for painting because ____

____

The paper that was best for writing was ________________________

It was the best for writing because ______________________________________

____

____

The paper that was best for mopping up water was ________________________

It was the best for mopping up water because ____________________________

____

____

In this lesson I learnt how to investigate by ______________________________

____

____

Key learning

In this lesson I have learnt that: Paper is a **manufactured material**. It is made from wood, which is a **natural** material. Different types of paper have different **properties**. For example, some are more **absorbent** than others. Some types of paper can be **reused** or **recycled**, and some cannot.

Homework

How many different types of paper can you find at home? Talk to a parent or adult about how you could use less paper, and reuse or recycle as much as possible.

Lesson 4 Is all fabric the same?

Key vocabulary

material
natural
property/properties
recycle
reuse

Activity 1: Describing fabrics

- Examine each fabric.
- Use your senses of sight and touch.
- Choose one fabric.
- Draw a circle around the words that describe it.

You will need

- samples of different types of fabrics

soft warm strong
thin rough fluffy
dark thick smooth
shiny colourful patterned
scratchy silky light
bright stretchy

Write the name of the fabric. ______________________

Write what type of clothes the fabric would be good for and why. Use the words above to help.

____

____

Activity 2: What can you see?

- Look at each fabric with the magnifier.
- Name an item of clothing it might be used for.

You will need

- samples of three different types of fabrics (for example with a distinctive weave or pattern)
- a magnifier

	Sample 1	Sample 2	Sample 3
What it looks like through a magnifier			
An item of clothing it might be used for			

Activity 3: Reusing and recycling fabric

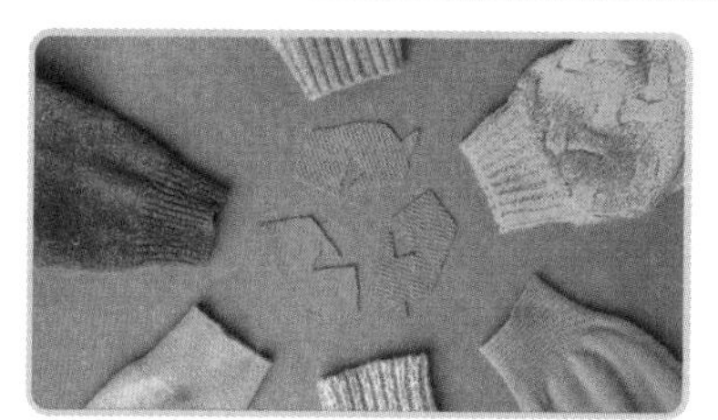

Clothes can often be reused or recycled.

Give one example of what you could do with an old item of clothing:

____

____

Key learning

In this lesson I have learnt that: Fabric is a manufactured **material**. Some fabrics are made from **natural** materials, such as wool. Some fabric is made from **recycled** material. Different types of fabric have different **properties**. Fabric should be **reused** or recycled whenever possible.

Homework

Look for different types of fabric at home. Talk to a parent or carer about how you could use reuse or recycle unwanted clothes.

Lesson 5 How can we group objects made of different materials?

Key vocabulary

manufactured material natural

Activity 1: Natural or manufactured?

Decide whether each material is natural or manufactured. Draw a circle around the correct word.

wood

natural manufactured

metal

natural manufactured

plastic

natural manufactured

glass

natural manufactured

rock

natural manufactured

brick

natural manufactured

water

natural manufactured

paper

natural manufactured

fabric

natural manufactured

Activity 2: Objects made from more than one material

- Look at each of your objects.
- Write its name in the table.
- Tick (✓) to show which materials it is made from.
- Two examples are shown.

You will need

- objects made from more than one material

	wood	plastic	metal	glass	rock	brick	water	paper	fabric
scissors		✓	✓						
pop-up toy	✓	✓	✓						

Activity 3: Sorting objects

Look at these objects. Decide if they are made from metal or plastic or both.

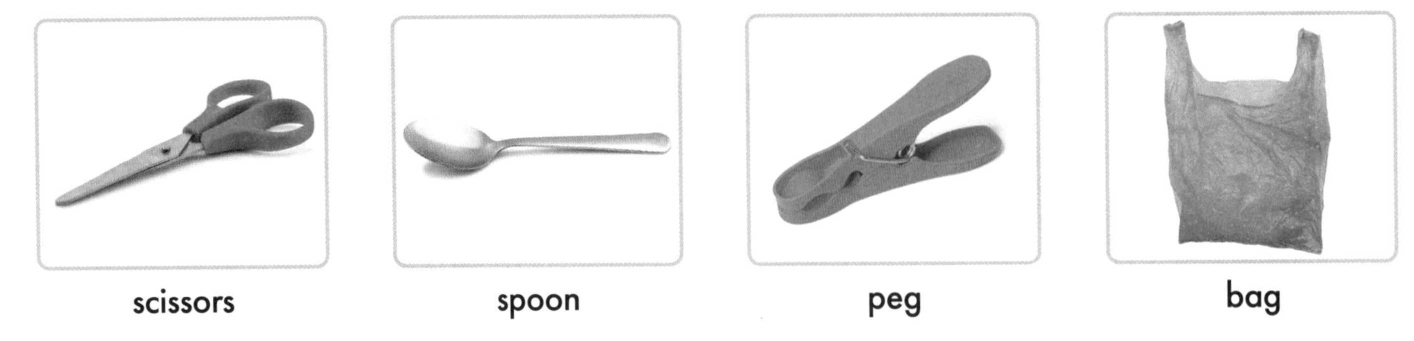

- Write the names or draw the objects in the correct part of the sorting hoops.
- Add one more object into each part of the sorting hoops.

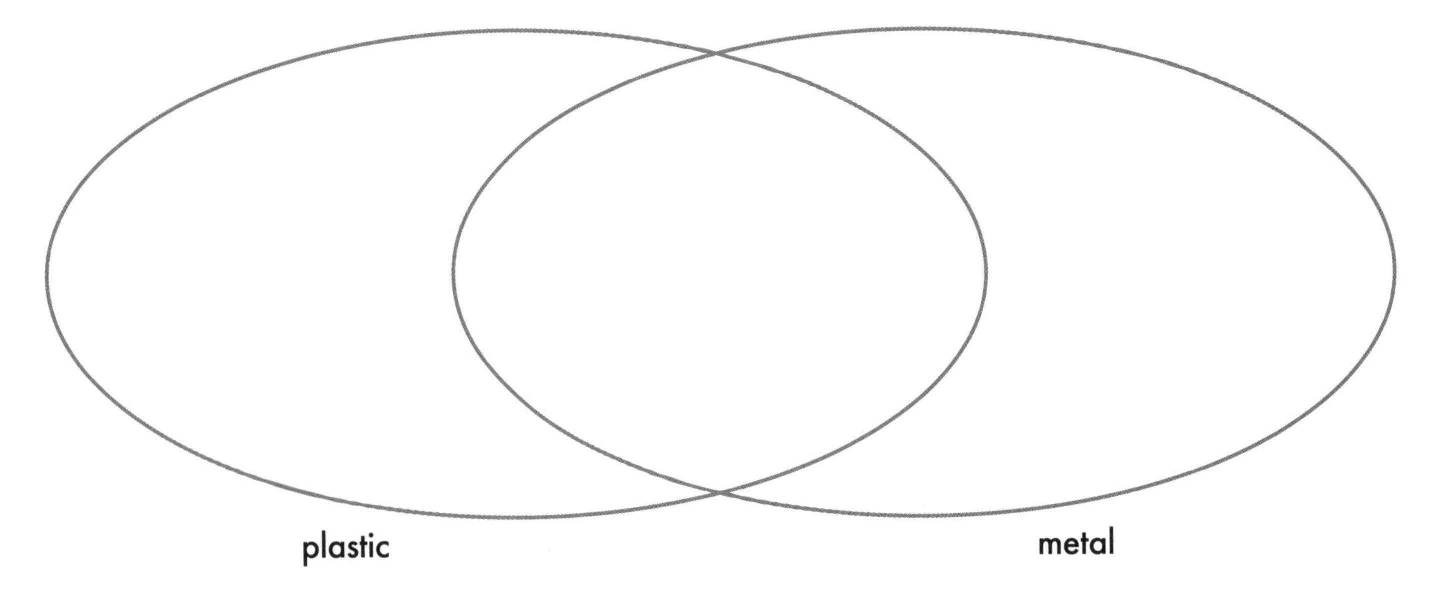

Key learning

In this lesson I have learnt that: We can sort objects into groups according to the materials they are made from. Materials can be **natural** or **manufactured**. Objects can be made from more than one **material**.

Homework

Find an object that is made of three or more different materials. Take a photograph or draw the object. Add labels to show the different materials.

Module 4

Properties and uses of materials

Lesson 1 Can the same object be made from different materials?

Key vocabulary

material property recycle reuse

Activity 1: What materials are they made from?

You will need

- four sets of the same type of object made from different materials

Why was this material chosen to make the object?

- Write the name of each type of object.
- Tick (✓) the materials they are made from. One has been started for you.
- Add one more material to the table.

	Cups			
Plastic	✓			
Paper				
Metal				

Choose one set of objects (for example, spoons). Complete this table for the set.

The objects I have chosen are all	
Material	**I think it was chosen because ...**

Activity 2: Which should I use?

A china

B reusable plastic

C single-use plastic

D paper

Look at the plates. Complete each sentence.

I think the best plate for a young child to use would be ____

I think the best plate to use on a picnic would be ____

I think the plate that is best for the environment is ____

I think the plate that is worst for the environment is ____

I think a material that would make a bad plate is ________________

Talk to a partner about your choices

Key learning

In this lesson I have learnt that: Objects are made from one or more **materials**. The **properties** of an object can be different from the properties of the material it is made from. Materials should be used carefully. They can often be **reused** or **recycled**.

Homework

Go on a 'hat hunt' in your home. Find as many hats as you can. Try to find hats made of different materials. Talk with a parent or carer about why different materials are used for hats. Bring a hat to the next lesson.

Lesson 2 What properties do materials have?

Key vocabulary

opaque property transparent

Activity 1: How does the material look and feel?

You will need

- samples of different materials

- Choose two materials. Write their names in the tables.
- Look at each material closely. Hold it to see how it feels.
- Choose property words from the box.
- Write them in the tables.

Material:	
Looks	**Feels**

Material:	
Looks	**Feels**

hard	soft	rough	smooth
shiny	dull	heavy	light
transparent	opaque	bendy	stretchy
flexible	rigid		

Activity 2: What material is it?

You will need

- samples of different materials
- a drawstring bag

- Hide a material in the bag.
- Talk to a partner about the material.
- Ask your partner to guess what the material is.
- Take the material out of the bag and look at it together.
- Write the name of the material in all the boxes it matches.
- Repeat for other materials.

Names of materials:

wood	metal
plastic	glass
rock	brick
water	paper
fabric	

Hard	Soft	Rough	Smooth	Shiny
Dull	**Heavy**	**Light**	**Transparent**	**Opaque**

Key learning

In this lesson I have learnt that: Materials have **properties** that make them useful for different purposes. For example, glass is **transparent**, which makes it useful for windows. Brick is **opaque**, which makes it useful for walls.

Homework

Look for some transparent materials at home. Try to find two or three different objects.

Lesson 3 Does it bend or stretch?

Key vocabulary

bar chart
bend
flexible
property
rigid
stretch
test

Activity 1: Stretch test

You will need

- three different socks
- six coloured strips of paper
- scissors
- large sheet of paper
- glue
- a camera (optional)

You will do a **test** to see if socks stretch.

1. Cut a paper strip as long as the sock. Label the paper strip 'Sock 1'. Stretch the sock.
2. Cut a paper strip as long as the sock now. Label the paper strip 'Sock 1 after stretching'. Do the same for Sock 2 and Sock 3.
3. Stick the paper strips side by side to create a **bar chart**.
4. Stick a photograph in the box or draw your chart. If you measured the paper strips with a ruler, write your results in the table.

	Before stretching	After stretching
Sock 1		
Sock 2		
Sock 3		

Activity 2: Test results

Complete the sentences.

When we stretched the socks they ______________________________

When we stopped stretching the socks they ______________________________

The sock that stretched the most was ______________________________

The sock that stretched the least was ______________________________

Activity 3: Flexible or rigid?

Flexible materials can bend without breaking. Rigid materials cannot bend without breaking.

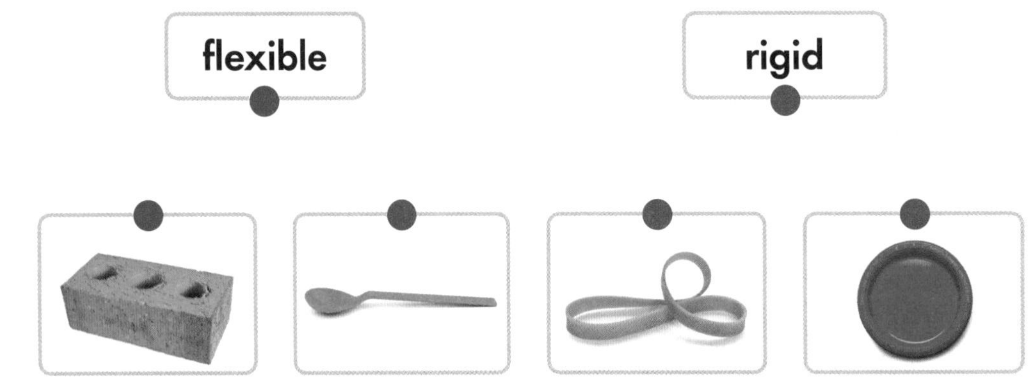

Draw lines to show which objects are flexible and which objects are rigid.

Can you think of any other objects made from a rigid material?

____

Key learning

In this lesson I have learnt that: Some materials can **stretch**. Some are **flexible**: they can **bend** without breaking. Others are **rigid**: they cannot bend or stretch. Each **property** is useful for different purposes.

Homework

Test some of your socks at home. Find out which socks are the most stretchy.

Lesson 4 Do all materials get wet?

Key vocabulary

absorb/absorbent   property   waterproof

Activity 1: Absorbency test

You will need

- samples of four different fabrics
- a transparent beaker
- a water dropper
- water

You are going to carry out a test.

- Place a piece of fabric on top of the beaker.
- Carefully drop water onto the fabric.
- Draw or write your results in the correct column, or stick in a piece of the fabric.

waterproof water stays on the surface or runs off	**absorbent** water soaks in	**not absorbent** water goes through into the beaker

Activity 2: Waterproof or absorbent?

Draw a circle around the correct sentence.

All materials get wet.

Not all materials get wet.

I know this because ______________________________

____

When water falls on a waterproof fabric ______________________________

____

Waterproof fabric is good for ______________________________

____

When water falls on an absorbent fabric ______________________________

____

Absorbent fabric is good for ______________________________

____

In this lesson I learnt how to ______________________________

____

Key learning

In this lesson I have learnt that: Some materials are **absorbent**: they soak up water. Some are **waterproof**: they do not let water pass through. Each **property** is useful for different purposes.

Homework

Look for waterproof and absorbent materials at home. Find out what they are used for.

Module 5

Animals (vertebrates)

Lesson 1 Who's who in the animal world?

Key vocabulary

amphibian	bird	fish	reptile
backbone	diet	mammal	vertebrate

Activity 1: What makes a reptile a reptile?

Which animals do you know? Do you know any that don't have fur?

There are five vertebrate groups of animals. Amphibians, mammals, reptiles, birds and fish. Vertebrates have a backbone.

These four animals are reptiles. How are they the same and how are they different?

green iguana

Hermann's tortoise

Nile crocodile

corn snake

Use the pictures and the words in the box to complete the sentences.

A reptile is a ____________________

All vertebrates have a ____________________

All reptiles have ____________________

Most reptiles have ____________________

Some reptiles have ____________________

Most reptiles live on ____________________

scaly skin
claws
legs
land
vertebrate
backbone

Activity 2: How do I know it is a reptile?

Look at the pictures and complete the sentences below. Think about how it looks, where it lives, what it eats and if it lays eggs.

I can tell that this crocodile is a reptile because ______________________________

____

____

I can tell that this snake is a reptile because ______________________________

____

____

Do all reptiles eat the same diet? Tick (✓) one. Yes ☐ No ☐

Key learning

In this lesson I have learnt that: In the animal kingdom, there are five **vertebrate** groups: **reptiles**, **birds**, **amphibians**, **fish** and **mammals**. Vertebrates have a **backbone**. Reptiles have scaly skin and lay eggs. Most live on land and have teeth and claws. Different reptiles have different **diets**.

Homework

Find out about two other reptiles. Find out what they eat.

Lesson 2 What's so special about birds?

Key vocabulary

beak	claws	feathers	omnivore
bird	diet	herbivore	wings
carnivore	eggs		

Activity 1: What do birds have in common?

Which birds have you seen?
Are all birds the same?

These four animals are birds. How are they the same and how are they different?

chicken

sparrow

emperor penguin

barn owl

Use the pictures and the words to complete the sentences.

These birds are similar because ______________________________

____

These birds are different because ______________________________

____

Activity 2: What makes a bird a bird?

gull

kestrel

pigeon

Use the pictures and the words in the box to complete the sentences.

beak	claws
eggs	feathers
fly	swim
wings	

All birds have ______________________________

All birds lay ______________________________

Most birds can ______________________________

Some birds can ______________________________

Activity 3: What do birds eat?

Draw lines to complete the sentences.

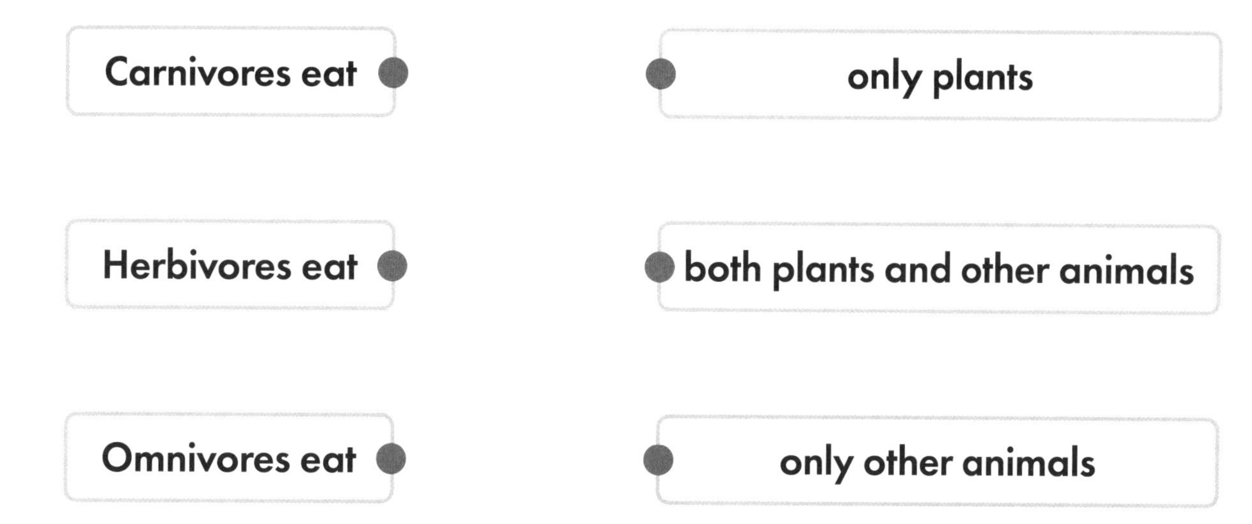

Write the word carnivore, herbivore or omnivore for each bird.

Bird	Eats	Carnivore, herbivore or omnivore?
swan		
budgerigar		
barn owl		

Key learning

In this lesson I have learnt that: **Birds** have **beaks**, **claws**, **wings** and **feathers**. They lay **eggs**, and most can fly. Their **diet** varies; some are **carnivores**, some are **herbivores** and some are **omnivores**.

Homework

Look for birds near your home. Find out what types of birds they are.

Lesson 3 What makes an amphibian an amphibian?

Key vocabulary

amphibian	diet	herbivore	spawn
carnivore	froglet/newtlet/toadlet	lungs	tadpole

Activity 1: What do amphibians have in common?

common toad

common frog

smooth newt

red-eyed tree frog

Which amphibians do you know? Where have you seen them? What are they like?

Use the pictures to complete the sentences.

These amphibians are similar because ______________________________

____

These amphibians are different because ______________________________

____

____

Activity 2: Life stages of amphibians

Look at the life stages of these two amphibians and read the information below.

Common frog

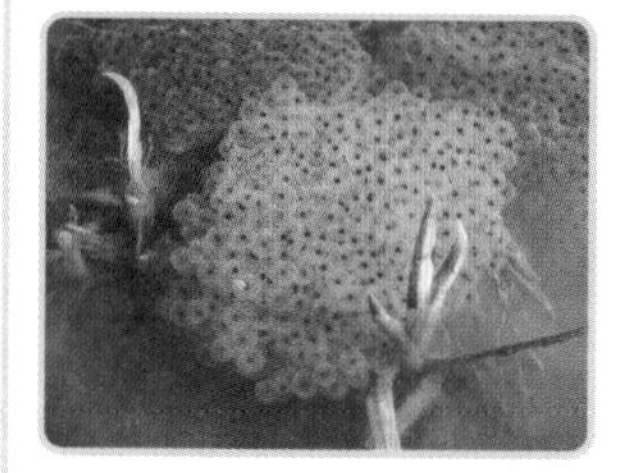
spawn

tadpole (herbivore)

froglet (carnivore)

adult (carnivore)

Smooth newt

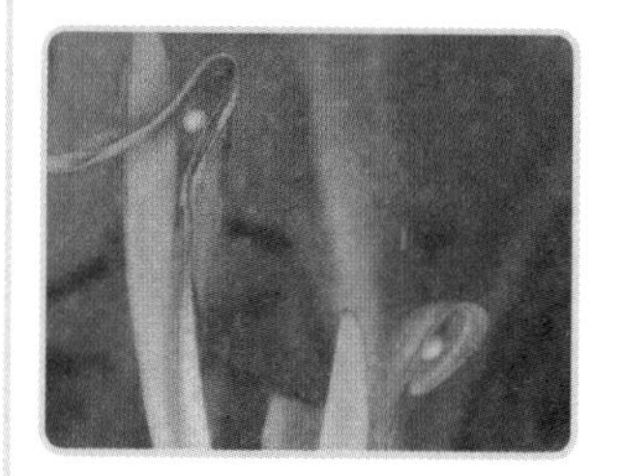
spawn

tadpole (herbivore)

newtlet (carnivore)

adult (carnivore)

Amphibians change during their life. They start on or in the water and end as adults living near water but mainly on land. They can swim and breathe underwater when they are young and develop **lungs** for breathing air on land as they grow up.

What amphibians eat can change in its life. Common frogs are herbivores when they are **tadpoles**, but become carnivores when they are **froglets**.

Write carnivore and herbivore in the correct places in the table.

	Common frog	Smooth newt
tadpole		
froglet/newtlet		
adult		

Activity 3: The Common toad

Common toad

spawn

tadpole (herbivore)

toadlet (carnivore)

adult (carnivore)

Look at the pictures and complete the sentence.

I can tell that a toad is an amphibian because ______________________________

____

____

Match the toad's life stages to its diet.

tadpole

toadlet

adult

small animals such as worms and insects

water plants

Key learning

In this lesson I have learnt that: **Amphibians** lay eggs and live on land and in water. Their **diet** changes with their changing stages of life. They usually start life as **herbivores** then become **carnivores**.

Homework

Find out about two more amphibians. Find out where they live and what they eat at different stages of their life.

Lesson 4 Do fish have fingers?

Key vocabulary

carnivore	eye	gills	scales
diet	fin	herbivore	tail
eggs	fish	omnivore	

Activity 1: What do fish have in common?

rainbow trout

hammerhead shark

Which fish do you know? Where have you seen them? What are they like?

clownfish

king salmon

Look at the pictures and complete the sentences.

These fish are similar because ______________________________

____

These fish are different because ______________________________

____

Activity 2: Parts of a fish

- Label the parts of this goldfish.
- Use the words in the box.

Complete the sentences.

All fish have ______________________________

All fish lay ______________________________

All fish live in the ______________________________

Did you know that most fish have teeth? They're not always easy to see!

Look at a real fish. Draw and label a picture of it here.

Activity 3: What do fish eat?

Look at what each fish eats. Write **carnivore**, or **omnivore** for each fish.

Fish	Eats	Carnivore or omnivore?
hammerhead shark		
king salmon		
goldfish		

Key learning

In this lesson I have learnt that: **Fish** have **gills**, **fins** and a **tail**, and most have **scales**. They live in water and they lay **eggs**. Different fish have different **diets**.

Homework

Next time you are in a shop that sells whole fish, name the parts you can see and say what is the same and what is different about them.

Lesson 5 Are humans mammals?

Key vocabulary

birth	fur	milk
carnivore	herbivore	offspring
diet	mammal	omnivore

Activity 1: What is a mammal?

Look at these mammals.

tiger

cow

giraffe

Look at the features in the table. Tigers, cows, giraffes and other mammals have these features.

Tick (✓) the features that a human has.

	Tiger	Cow	Giraffe	Human
Has hair or fur covering their bodies	✓	✓	✓	
Gives birth to live young	✓	✓	✓	
Makes milk for their offspring	✓	✓	✓	
Cares for their offspring	✓	✓	✓	
Offspring looks like a younger version of its parents	✓	✓	✓	

Activity 2: Carnivores, herbivores and omnivores

We can group animals by their diet.

carnivore herbivore omnivore

- Sort these animals into the correct groups.
- Write their names in the correct hoop.
- Add one more animal to each group.

tortoise

sparrow

adult frog

trout

rabbit

fox

Activity 3: This is a mammal because ...

Complete the sentences.

I can tell that a human is a mammal because ______________________________

____

____

____

____

____

These are giraffes. I can tell that a giraffe is a mammal, because ______________________________

____

____

____

____

____

Key learning

In this lesson I have learnt that: **Mammals** have hair or **fur**. They give **birth** to live young, then care for their **offspring** and make **milk** for them. Mammals' **diet** varies: they can be **carnivores, omnivores** or **herbivores**. Humans are mammals.

Homework

Think of some other mammals you know. Find out about their diet. Find out the name of the offspring and adult female.

Identifying plants and their parts

Lesson 1 What wild and garden plants can we find around our school?

Key vocabulary

flower garden leaf plant stem wild

Activity 1: Identifying wild and garden plants

How do you know if a plant is a garden plant or a wild plant?

What do plants need?

Look at the pictures or find plants near your school.

- Draw the plants in the boxes below, or take photographs and stick them in.
- Label the parts you know, such as root, **stem**, **flower** and **leaf**.

Wild plant	Garden plant
Name of plant: ______________________	Name of plant: ______________________

Activity 2: Wild or garden plants?

Match these plants to their names. Ask an adult to help you.

geranium **poppy** **petunia** **nettle**

- Draw a circle around the names of the wild plants.
- Underline the names of the garden plants.

Key learning

In this lesson I have learnt that: We can put **plants** into two groups: **wild** and **garden**. Wild plants grow without the help of people. Garden plants grow because people choose to plant them and take care of them.

Homework

Look out for flowers in storybooks at home or on the television. Draw or take photographs of any that you find.

Lesson 2 What parts of a plant grow above the ground?

Key vocabulary

flower leaf plant stem

Activity 1: Comparing plant parts

Look at the pictures.

- Compare the leaves, stems and flowers on the two plants.
- Choose one plant part.
- Draw a circle around the name of the part you have chosen.

leaves stems flowers

sunflower

nettle

Complete the sentences:

The ______________________________

on the two plants are similar because

____

____

The ______________________________

on the two plants are different because

____

____

Key learning

In this lesson I have learnt that: The parts of a flowering **plant** that grow above the ground are the **stem**, **leaves** and **flowers**. The parts of a plant can be different.

Homework

Look for plants around school or your home, or in books. Draw or take a photograph of your favourite plant. Think about what you like about the plant.

Lesson 3 What part of a plant grows under the ground?

Key vocabulary

branching roots plant roots tap root

Activity 1: Drawing root vegetables

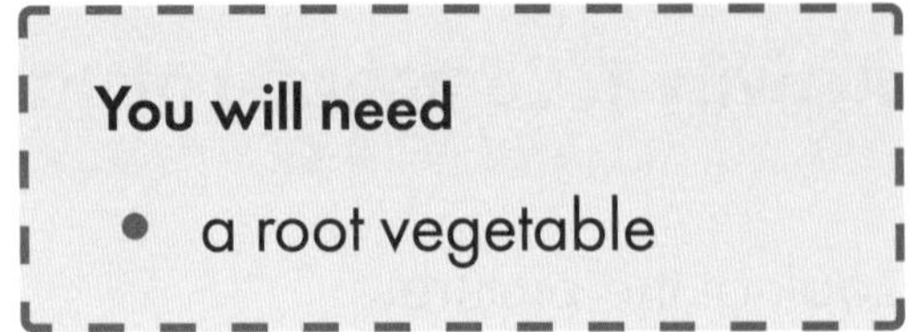

Look at these pictures of root vegetables growing in the ground. Use the questions to talk to your partner.

carrot plant

Which parts of the carrot plant are above the ground? Which parts are below the ground?

Which part of a root vegetable do we eat?

Draw another root vegetable growing in the ground. Show the stem and leaves pointing up. Show the root pointing down. Draw a line to show where the ground is.

Name of vegetable: ______________________

Activity 2: Tap roots and branching roots

- Look at the roots of these plants. Decide if the plants below have thick tap roots or thin branching roots.
- Draw lines to match the plants to the labels.

tap root

branching root

pasrnip

petunia

rose periwinkle

dandelion

tap root

branching root

Key learning

In this lesson I have learnt that: The part of a **plant** that grows below the ground is the **roots**. Some plants have many thin **branching roots**, and some have a one thick **tap root**.

Homework

Look at different vegetables in a shop. Decide if the part we eat is the root or not.

Why are trees plants?

Key vocabulary

bark	evergreen	leaf	roots	trunk
deciduous	flower	plant	stem	

Activity 1: Deciduous or evergreen?

Trees that lose their leaves are called **deciduous**. Trees that do not lose their leaves are called evergreen. **Evergreen** have green leaves all year.

Look at the pictures below. Circle the words deciduous or evergreen for each tree.

horse chestnut tree

summer winter

deciduous / evergreen

Scots pine tree

summer winter

deciduous / evergreen

Activity 2: Identifying trees

Look at the pictures and read the information about the trees.

Tree A

Tree B

Write A or B to show which tree is being written about.

Date palm tree (evergreen)

Leaves: long and thin with sharp, pointed tips.

Trunk: tall and straight with big bumps and spikes.

Flowers: white or pale yellow.

This is tree ____

Alder tree (deciduous)

Leaves: round with bumpy edges.

Trunk: tall and straight with cracks and rough patches.

Flowers: long, green or brown catkins.

This is tree ____

Activity 3: Parts of a tree

Is a tree a plant? Tick (✓) one. Yes ☐ No ☐

How do you know that a tree is a plant?
Talk with a partner using the words from the box.

flowers	leaves
roots	trunk (stem)

Key learning

In this lesson I have learnt that: Trees are **plants**. They have a **stem** (**trunk**), **leaves** and **roots**, and most have **flowers**.

Homework

Look for trees with flowers in books, films or as you are walking outside. Think of words that describe the flowers. Tell the class about the flowers you found on the tree.

Lesson 5 What are the similarities and differences between plants that have flowers?

Key vocabulary

flower leaf plant roots stem

Activity 1: Designing a plant

- Look at the photographs and find some more if possible.
- Choose your favourite root, stem, leaf and flower.
- Each part should come from a different plant.
- Put your favourite plant parts together to make a new plant. Draw it here.

above the ground branching roots flower leaf stem tap root trunk under the ground

- Label your drawing.
- Use words from the box.
- Label which plant each part came from.

Activity 2: Describing plant parts

- Describe the plant parts.
- Use the words in the box to help you.

branching	brown	curved	green
lines	long	pink	round
shiny	smooth	straight	tap
thick	thin		

oak tree

Describe these roots. ______________________

____

fig tree

Describe this leaf. ______________________

____

tulip

Describe this stem. ______________________

____

rose

Describe this flower. ______________________

____

Key learning

In this lesson I have learnt that: Different **plants** are similar because they all have **roots**, **stems** and **leaves**, and most have **flowers**. However, these parts look different on different plants.

Homework

Find out about a carnivorous plant. For example, a Venus fly trap or a pitcher plant.

William Collins' dream of knowledge for all began with the publication of his first book in 1819.
A self-educated mill worker, he not only enriched millions of lives, but also founded a flourishing publishing house. Today, staying true to this spirit, Collins books are packed with inspiration, innovation and practical expertise.
They place you at the centre of a world of possibility and give you exactly what you need to explore it.

Published by Collins
An imprint of HarperCollins*Publishers*
The News Building, 1 London Bridge Street, London, SE1 9GF, UK

HarperCollins*Publishers*
Macken House, 39/40 Mayor Street Upper, Dublin 1, D01 C9W8, Ireland

Browse the complete Collins catalogue at
collins.co.uk

10 9 8 7 6 5 4 3 2 1

ISBN 978-0-00-868322-1

British Library Cataloguing-in-Publication Data
A catalogue record for this publication is available from the British Library.

Development Editor: Sally Hillyer
Series Editor: Jane Turner
Consultant Reviewer: David Allen
Publisher: Laura White
Copyeditor: Sarah Snashall
Proofreader: Kariss Holgarth
Cover designer: Amparo at Kneath Associates
Packager: Oriel Square
Typesetter: Tech-Set
Production controller: Alhady Ali
Printed and bound in Great Britain by Martins the Printers

This book contains FSC™ certified paper and other controlled
sources to ensure responsible forest management.

For more information visit: www.harpercollins.co.uk/green

collins.co.uk/sustainability

Acknowledgements
This work is adapted from the original work, Snap Science Second Edition Year 1
All images are from Shutterstock, with the exception of p.45, right: Alamy – Pat Eyre

The publishers gratefully acknowledge the permission granted to reproduce the copyright material in this book. Every effort has been made to trace copyright holders and to obtain their permission for the use of copyright material. The publishers will gladly receive any information enabling them to rectify any error or omission at the first opportunity.